We Shoot Every Third Salesperson . . .

The Second One Just Left

Skills necessary for effective business-to-business telephone prospecting and account development

Winnie Ary
Ary Group, Inc.

KENDALL/HUNT PUBLISHING COMPANY
4050 Westmark Drive   Dubuque, Iowa 52002

This book is dedicated to my husband, Earl, who loves me without qualification or reservation and who provides the balance and stability in my life that is paramount to doing the work I love so much.

CONTENTS

PREFACE

Sales professionals who do not develop their telephone selling skills to be equal to their face-to-face skills may find themselves dinosaurs in today's market.

This book is written for and dedicated to all sales professionals who sell a product or service to any corporation, manufacturer, institution, association, school or organization. If your prospective customer is listed in the yellow pages, you need this book.

 What is the difference between the way we prospect and develop new business today vs. the way we did ten years ago?

 Now the biggest difference is that business decision makers don't want, and often won't allow, salespeople to walk into their office without a prescheduled appointment.

They have signs on the entrance doors stating, "No Solicitation," "Sales Professionals Seen by Appointment Only," and my favorite, **"We shoot every third salesperson . . . the second one just left!"** Today, it's considered intrusive and rude to "cold call" door to door in business to business sales.

Cold calling without an appointment sends a negative message to the decision maker.

1. The decision maker's work is so unimportant that it can be readily interrupted.
2. Whatever the salesperson has to say is so important that his/her convenience is more important than the decision maker's.

These assumptions certainly make the salesperson appear to be rude and inconsiderate.

Keep in mind, you're not the only one making cold, unannounced sales calls. You may follow the person who wants the decision maker to buy office equipment and supplies, join the chamber of commerce, sponsor the Special Olympics, have carpets cleaned, buy uniforms, select business insurance, and on and on. With all these "drop in" sales calls, business decision makers have become overwhelmed with a steady stream of traffic. That is why businesses today have gotten to the point that they say, *"We see sales people by appointment only. No solicitation!"* It's getting more and more difficult to walk in without an appointment so we must become proficient at building relationships by telephone. Yet, with most sales professionals, the use of the telephone for prospecting and developing new business is where they are the least effective.

While there are times when face to face cold calling may be appropriate, they should be infrequently. Dropping in unannounced should happen only when we're in the area and stop in to get a contact name, or drop off a business card or piece of literature.

 What else has changed in the past few years?

 Technology
- Electronic communications
- Fax machines
- Computers
- International trade
- Car phones
- Pagers
- Video teleconferencing
- The Internet—Web Pages

The world of professional sales has changed. Today, it is not cost effective to drive across town or to fly across the country to meet with a prospective customer just because he is willing to give the salesperson an appointment. In fact, one's prospective customer may be in another country.

As we become a more technologically oriented society, improvements in communications will greatly affect how we market our products and services. As communication systems continue to change, we will find the need for face-to-face sales calls greatly reduced. We'll combine face-to-face calls with the telephone when visual telephones become more affordable and as common as fax machines became in the late 1980s.

Fax machines went from a little known, little used item to a commodity almost over night and visual telephones will likely experience the same rapid acceptance. When visual telephones sit on everyone's desk, you will be displaying your proposals, demonstrating how other customers use your products and services, turning catalog pages and having prospects look at the same things you are looking at without leaving the office.

The need for excellent telephone skills will become even more critical as competition expands through telecommunications from local to global markets. Distance and time will become less and less of a sales obstacle.

The benefits of effective telephone prospecting for the dedicated sales professional include:

■ Being prepared in advance for every prospecting telephone call.
■ Techniques that confirm we have the true decision maker.
■ Knowledge of how to effectively fact-find and qualify to determine overall potential for business.
■ Using one's own and others' time more efficiently and effectively
■ Keeping the "funnel" full.

Consider the value of supplementing good face-to-face selling skills with the knowledge of how to effectively prospect, further develop existing accounts, and build long lasting relationships by telephone.

ACKNOWLEDGMENTS

For the encouragement and support of this book, I will be forever grateful to:

Joe Lozowski and Brad Steele, my heroes. Two of the finest sales executives in the country who encouraged me to write the book because they believed so much in my sales training techniques.

Angie Widmayer my administrative assistant who kept me organized, on schedule, and sane and who is always there when I need her.

Susan Schubert for her valuable assistance in helping me take my sales training materials and make them into a book.

All my wonderful clients and the many salespeople who over the years wrote and thanked me for my training and encouraged me to write a book.

My family for standing behind me and making me feel it was O.K. to seclude myself in my office on weekends and holidays to work on the book.

Last but not least my friend, Nan Worthington, who in 1988 said to me, "Go for it! You're good, you can do it."

ABOUT THIS BOOK

 Who will benefit from using this book?

 Those engaged in selling a product or service to other businesses.

This book is based on the sales training program I wrote in 1993 entitled Prospecting and Developing New Business (PDNB.) The program has been presented, with great results, to clients such as Steelcase Inc., Ashland Chemical, Huntington National Bank, Sprint, and Allied International.

I wrote this book because I know what it is like to look at the "sales funnel" and feel the panic associated with finding it empty or "low on fuel." Even seasoned sales professionals, like myself, experience the "empty funnel" feeling on occasions. Why does that happen to even the most experienced sales professional? Because when it comes to picking up the telephone to prospect for business, we resist. We hate making cold calls. We procrastinate, hoping that if we wait long enough, something will happen on its own, and, our most serious offense, we don't prepare.

Most salespeople have never had any quality training in how to prospect. Many who did have training felt the old-style techniques they were taught bordered on unprofessional and deceptive tactics or the training consisted of playing the infamous numbers game in which you make 100 calls to get ten nibbles to get two appointments to close one sale. The numbers game, often referred to as "slam dunking," ultimately results in severe burnout for most sales professionals. Most of us view prospecting by telephone as an unpleasant, almost unethical task.

When I was in sales management, I encouraged and trained my staff to use the telephone to prospect and prequalify business opportunities. In addition to managing outside sales, I developed and managed several business to business telemarketing departments that went one step further than appointment setting. They sold and serviced their own accounts by phone. At that time, closing sales by phone was perceived as difficult, at best, to totally impossible because most sales training focused on using the telephone strictly for the purpose of gaining an appointment. Sales managers and sales professionals believed, as some still do today, you must meet face to face to develop rapport. This is just not true!

In business today, we have a vast number of decision makers who grew up with technology and developed the habit of using the phone to conduct business. By comparison, 10 to 15 years ago, a salesperson would have called the prospective customer and said something like this:

Hello Jason, This is Eric at the Smith Company. I was wondering if you might have just a few minutes to see me later today or in the morning. There were a couple of things on the proposal I neglected to mention yesterday during our meeting and I would like to go over them with you. What time is best for you?

By contrast, today Eric would call and say the following:

Jason, This is Eric with the Smith Company. If you've got that proposal handy I was wondering if we could just take a minute and address something I overlooked yesterday. Is this a good time?

Business is conducted more efficiently by phone today and, if you know what you are doing, the results can be an increase in sales as well as the development of many meaningful and professional relationships.

The techniques presented in this book can be customized by the user and easily applied to his particular environment. Written expressly for the professional salesperson to use independently as well as for the sales trainer, the content of this practical, "how to" book includes using the telephone as a vital sales tool, preparing for telephone prospecting, selling to the right person, the decision maker, asking for the business or opportunity, listening to and addressing resistant responses, determining overall potential for business, and the using of documentation for follow-up and building relationships.

Each chapter builds upon the previous one so it is best to read each chapter in sequential order. Most of these skills apply to in person appointments as well as they do to telephone conversations or, as I refer to them, **telephone appointments.**

I have the reputation as a trainer/consultant with a hard hitting, no nonsense, show no mercy style. My sales training sessions are often referred to as "sweaty palms" workshops. This book is written in that same style. Every chapter has explanations, examples, sample scripts, or exercises enabling the serious sales professional to improve rapidly and achieve goals—making money for himself, profit for his company and servicing the customer with the right products and services.

As you read the book, you will not find trickery and unethical methods suggested for business to business telephone prospecting. You will find telephone prospecting techniques that anyone can feel comfortable using and that have been proven to be enormously successful.

There's no such thing as a born salesperson. Super star sales professionals are not good just because they have great personalities or the gift of gab. The ones that make it to the top are the ones who have developed their skills through practice and commitment. The right choice of words and the most effective qualifying or closing techniques to use have become as natural as breathing. They become learned behaviors. Through practice and commitment, the selling skills or "competencies" are mastered and committed to memory. What's the difference between those who earn the big dollars in sales and those who struggle? Selling Skills.

Allow yourself no mercy as you conscientiously improve your telephone prospecting skills. Capitalize on your own drive, motivation, and desire to succeed.

The telephone is not a tool to make an appointment . . . it **is** an appointment.

Winnie Ary

Getting Started— Preparation

1

How do you think most business people feel today about doing more business by phone as opposed to scheduling in person appointments? How does it benefit them?

They find the telephone an efficient means of conducting business because of one or more of the following:

- It saves time.
- It saves money. (Time is money!)
- Convenience. They get more information more quickly.
- Business people feel less threatened. On the phone, it's easier to get rid of the salesperson.

How does it benefit the salesperson?

The telephone is an efficient means of conducting business because of one or more of the following:

- It saves time.
- It saves money. (Time is money!)

- Convenience. They get more information more quickly.
- Because the decision maker feels less threatened, they are usually more receptive to talking.

Field sales calls are expensive. The cost of the average field call has tripled in the past few years. Without proper prequalifying, not only is the face-to-face sales call costly, but, often, a total waste of time. As such, calling on a prospective customer just because they were (a) willing to see you and (b) breathing and have a pulse, is no longer acceptable. We need to make sure we are working smart as well as hard.

How do I mentally prepare for the "hang-ups?"

When you make business-to-business telephone prospecting calls in a professional and appropriate manner, "hang ups" will rarely happen.

First of all, keep in mind you are not "Tillie Telemarketer," calling people at home during the dinner hour trying to sell them waterproofing for their basements or magazine subscriptions. You are a professional salesperson calling a business person. It will be rare that anyone just hangs up on you. A blatant hang up will be just as rare as an immediate sale. What you are more likely to hear is something like this:

- You caught me at a bad time.
- I have a meeting starting in five minutes.
- I've got another call on hold.
- Just send me something in the mail.

Later in the book, we address how to effectively deal with typically heard points of resistance or objections. In the meantime, keep in mind that business people have telephones on their desks for a reason. It's one of the ways they conduct business.

Take a minute and look at your current telephone prospecting / selling skills. Rate your skills. 5—Very good, 4—good, 3—average, 2—poor, 1—very poor.

1. How do you compare your telephone prospecting and selling skills to your in-person selling skills?

    (a) My current in-person selling skills are: 5 4 3 2 1
    (b) My current telephone prospecting / selling
        skills are: 5 4 3 2 1

2. How does your company rate the importance of telephone selling skills in comparison to in-person selling skills?

    (a) In-person skills are considered: 5 4 3 2 1
    (b) Telephone prospecting / selling skills
        are considered: 5 4 3 2 1

3. How do you rate the importance of telephone skills in comparison to in-person sales skills?

    (a) I consider the importance of in person sales
        skills a: 5 4 3 2 1
    (b) I consider the importance of telephone
        selling skills a: 5 4 3 2 1

If in any area your rating was below five, improvement or a change in attitude is needed. To compete in todays hyper, competitive and very technical society we must have good prospecting skills on the phone as well as in person. Anything less puts us at a distinct disadvantage. Far too much business today is conducted by telephone for any sales professional to have anything less than excellent telephone selling skills.

What usually inspires or motivates sales professionals to get on the phone and prospect?

Their numbers are not on target, the funnel is empty, they want to increase their income.

Here is a typical situation:

The boss comes to you and says, "Daren, your numbers are not looking good. You're not going to make quota this quarter." The shivers go up and down your spine and you feel the stress that only a sales professional knows when sales are not where they need to be. You go to your desk and say, "I've got to get on the phone and get some appointments. I've got to find some business."

You start digging out your collection of business cards, inactive account lists, or anything you can get your hands on that will provide you with names and telephone numbers. Sound familiar?

You waste 30 or 40 minutes with multiple trips to the coffee pot and the restroom, and you've engaged in casual conversation with anybody and everybody who will take the time. You are into serious procrastination. Finally, you decide you must get on the phone.

You start shuffling through the cards and papers while mumbling under your breath. . . .

I don't think they'll be interested.
I heard they're in financial trouble.
They're probably too small to buy anything.
I bet everybody calls on them, they're huge.
Here's one I might try.

You're sitting there praying, "Dear God, please let the phone ring and let it be someone who wants to buy something right now." You would give almost anything if your manager would say to you, "Here's fourteen companies I want you to contact A.S.A.P. They are interested in doing business with us." Life would be good, but it doesn't happen that way.

Q. When I'm ready to begin telephone prospecting, how do I decide who to call first?

A. Come in early, stay late, skip lunch but have that decision made before you sit down to make calls.

When sales people need to prospect, they typically resist, procrastinate and they don't prepare.

Get your prospect calling list ready in advance. Unless you prepare in advance, it will be like Christmas shopping in the Mall of America for half a dozen people with no idea what they want or need. You'll go crazy, waste time, and your brain will glaze over with the enormous effort.

The complexity of your product or service and market potential will dictate the number of names you will initially need on your prospecting list. However, 25 to 35 is usually a good number for a start. In some cases, you will not be calling that person or company for the first time. Many prospecting calls are follow-up calls rather than first time cold calls. You'll find that your list will grow with time.

Next, schedule time for prospecting by physically marking the day and the hours allocated on your weekly planner. Treat that time with the same sanctity and dedication as an appointment with a customer.

Some sales professionals will dance around a dental or hair appointment like nothing you've ever seen in order to avoid rescheduling. Both their dentist and hair stylists are highly sought after and booked 4 to 6 weeks in advance. Heaven forbid, if we would not get our teeth cleaned or our hair styled on a timely basis. Yet, with the blink of an eye, we will give away time allocated for prospecting which incidentally provides the income necessary to pay the dentist and the hair stylist.

Q. How much time do we need to allocate when we schedule telephone prospecting.

 A. At least 1.5 to 2.0 hours per scheduled session.

You need at least that much time to build momentum and enthusiasm. Prospecting takes time and energy. You must stay with it for long enough to produce results. No pain, no gain. Don't think taking that 15 to 20 minutes before you need to leave for an appointment will suffice. It won't. The likelihood of finding gold after panning for 15 to 20 minutes is storybook material. In the real world, it rarely happens that way.

Take your prospecting time seriously and guard it with a passion. Notify the front desk or call your secretary or administrative support. Use your voice mail. Make it clear to yourself as well as others that you will not be taking calls during allocated prospecting time unless it is an emergency.

I've done quite a bit of consulting in the office furniture industry over the years and I've said this a hundred times. "Nobody ever died on the way to the hospital because their furniture did not arrive on time." Unless you are in the business of selling heart transplants, don't take calls during precious prospecting time. No excuses. It's only a couple of hours.

 Q. What is the worst time to schedule prospecting calls?

 A. Monday morning.

What are you like on Monday morning? Statistics indicate most business decision makers are least receptive to receiving unsolicited sales calls on Monday morning. Even if there are some who don't mind, why play the odds?

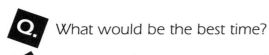

Q. What would be the best time?

A. Actually, any time other than Monday morning can be good.

Some will argue that Friday afternoon is a total loss because decision makers and business owners knock off early to get a head start on the weekend. I tend to disagree. I've found Fridays can be most productive. While I agree you may find fewer decision makers available, ones that are in are often more receptive to your call. They are often mellow, relaxed, and looking forward to the weekend. Next week's schedule of things to do seems light years away. Don't discount the value of making prospecting calls on Friday afternoon.

Prospect when you are at your best. Prospect when you are at your highest energy level, not when you are in "low gear." I'm a morning person. My feet hit the floor at 5:30–6:00 a.m. and I'm a ball of energy. At about 3.00 p.m., I start to fizzle out as my energy drains. I know that about myself.

Therefore, my best prospecting time is morning. When are you at your best? Consider that when allocating time for prospecting.

TIME TO PROSPECT

	Mon	Tue	Wed	Thur	Fri
A.M.	✕	✓	*9 - 11* Prospect ✓	✓	✓
P.M.	✓	✓	✓	✓	♡

Worst time to prospect **Monday Morning**

Best time to prospect **My choice**

Amount of prospecting time to allocate per session **1½- 2 hrs.**

Number of *qualifying conversations per hour **4 -6**

Notes: **I'm a morning person. Do mornings.**
Thur. No good. Sales meetings

The results of consistent and effective telephone prospecting is new business on a regular basis and less peaks and valleys.

Winnie Ary

How many effective "telephone appointments" or qualifying conversations can you expect to complete in one hour?

 Four to Six.

You may make 15 to 20 calls (connects), but you will be exceptional if you are able to have more than four to six qualifying conversations in an hour. Between the not-ins, voice mail messages, and re-directs to another person, four to six qualifying calls is a reasonable expectation.

 What is a qualifying conversation?

 A qualifying conversation provides enough information to determine overall potential for business and the appropriate next step.

Appropriate steps or actions for follow-ups can include: sending information, scheduling a time to call back and scheduling an appointment to meet. On the other hand, the conversation could provide enough information for you to dead file this as a non-qualified lead with little or no future potential.

 What's the most effective way to keep the funnel full?

 Allocate time to make prospecting calls and don't give up that time unless absolutely necessary.

Successful salespeople live, die and breath by prospecting and keeping their prospect funnel full. Let's assume you commit to allocating two hours each week for telephone prospecting and average four qualifying conversations per hour. That means in one week, you may talk to and begin, or continue, the **"wooing"** process with eight potential new customer's per week. (We'll talk more about the "wooing" process later in this book.)

Multiply this by four weeks in a month and you've had 32 opportunities (time saving, productive telephone appointments) with which to gain new accounts, or at least, gain additional ground. This is what keeps the peaks and valleys of sales to a minimum. This is what insures continuous sales and lofty commission checks.

 Will I need to telephone prospect forever to insure always having a full funnel?

 That depends on the nature of your business.

Keep the Funnel Full!

If you sell a product or service that is a one time or infrequent sale, then you will need to spend more time prospecting than the sales professional that lands an account and receives ongoing, repeat business. For example, selling a new roof to a building owner is likely to happen once every 15 to 20 years. On the other hand, landing an account that commits to using your payroll and accounting service is ongoing, repeat business.

There are many ways to find new business in addition to telephone prospecting. Networking, advertising, direct mail, tips clubs, referrals, and sponsorships, are some examples. However, in business to business selling, at some point a phone call will be necessary. When you have mastered the skills necessary to be effective at telephone prospecting, you will never again worry about how to find new business. You will also never again worry about earning an above average income because businesses want and need good "hunters." Hunters don't wait for business, they go after it.

Those of us in sales know very well what peaks and valleys mean. One day we are on top of the mountain with a lot going for us and then, suddenly, we have closed or lost every opportunity and we're back in the valley. This happens when we

(a) neglect to prospect on a regular basis and/or
(b) when we do, our attempts are ineffective.

We can change that!

KEY POINTS FOR CHAPTER ONE

■ Come in early, stay late, skip lunch but have your call list ready in advance.

■ Set aside one and one-half to two hours for effective telephone prospecting on a regular basis and schedule the time in your weekly planner. Protect the time at all cost.

■ Avoid making first time prospecting calls on Monday morning, schedule yourself when you are at your best, and don't discount the value of calling Friday afternoons.

■ Expect to complete four to six qualifying conversations per hour.

■ Keep the prospecting funnel full to avoid peaks and valleys in sales.

Effective
Salespeople
Are Essential
. . . Not Optional.

Winnie Ary

Determine
Decision Maker 2

 Should the objective of a telephone prospecting call be exclusively to get an appointment?

 NO! NO! NO! The purpose should be to get a **qualified** appointment.

Better yet, the purpose should be to position ourselves to make a sale or gain an account. Remember, in many situations, just because a potential buyer is breathing, has a pulse and is willing to see you is not justification for a sales call. Anyone who has been in sales for six months or more knows how it feels to be sitting in a decision makers office saying to yourself, "Why am I here? This account has no potential."

Most traditional sales training teaches the sales professional to focus on getting the appointment. The instructions were to get the appointment, at any cost. Nothing else mattered. It was as if we believed there was magic associated with meeting in person, eyeball to eyeball, handshake to handshake. The clouds were expected to part, rays of light were supposed to emerge, and doves were expected to appear with signed orders clutched in their claws. Miracles were expected to happen when we met face to face that just couldn't happen by phone.

Today, people build very meaningful business relationships by phone prior to meeting personally. In some cases, the phone relationship makes the personal meeting unnecessary, as many companies today have turned to selling exclusively by phone.

Don't Kiss on the First Date

I know this sounds somewhat old fashioned, but compare telephone prospecting to a first date. To make an important point, let's pretend that mother has warned, **"Don't kiss on the first date."** Generally, we'll spend some time getting to know each other, determining common denominators, and maybe even have dinner, lunch, or a drink after work. Then, later in the date, if all goes well, you kiss. Assuming you have established good rapport and understanding, the kiss is well received. If not, it may be that you rushed the process and your date went into the "resistance mode".

How do you think a prospective customer feels about receiving a telephone call from a salesperson who rattles a speech off in 60 seconds about their company, their product or their service, and then asks for an appointment? You've done very little rapport building and there were no questions about their business or service or what is important to them. In other words, a kiss is planted without the initial "wooing." No wonder we face such "rejection" when making those types of telephone prospecting calls.

What steps are necessary in making successful telephone prospecting calls?

1. Get the name,
2. Get the position, and
3. Get them on the phone.

There is a poem or story about a child who proudly announced he was going to eat an elephant. His friend incredulously asked how that could be possible because it's so humongous. The child responded, One bite at a time."

That is exactly how sales professionals should tackle telephone prospecting and new business development. One bite, or one step at a time.

1. Get the name.

By having the name, you have an advantage. If they are not available now, you can call again later and ask for them by name. Don't forget the value of asking for their extension or direct dial number.

2. Get their position.

Knowing their position or title assures you are targeting the appropriate decision-maker. You are not looking for the order placer; you are seeking the order maker.

(Note: Typically you will get better results asking for their position rather than title, particularly in smaller corporations.)

3. Get them on the phone.

At least attempt to get them on the phone. Almost as an afterthought, ask to speak with them.

Let's look at how a typical telephone prospecting call has been done in the past:

RECEPTIONIST: *Good morning, Holiday Boat Repair.*

SALESPERSON: *Hello, this is Don Bright with Contract Chemicals. I'd like to talk to the person who purchases chemicals for your shop. Would they be available?*

RECEPTIONIST: *May I tell him the purpose of your call?*

SALESPERSON: *Sure, I just wanted to see if I could talk to him about his chemical needs and see if we could be of service.*

RECEPTIONIST: *Just a moment and I'll see if he's available.*

(Placed on hold for 2 minutes listening to elevator music.)

RECEPTIONIST: *Sir, our purchasing department said to tell you they are not interested in changing suppliers at this time but if you would like to send your catalog and pricing information they would be happy to keep it on file.*

SALESPERSON: *Ok, who would I send that to?*

RECEPTIONIST: *Just send it to the attention of purchasing. Our address is 1301 East Jefferson Avenue, etc.*

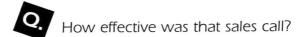 How effective was that sales call?

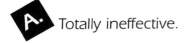 Totally ineffective.

Why do you think we did not get through on the phone? Why do sales people get blocked so often on the initial phone contact? Are you using this approach?

I'd like to talk to the person who takes care of . . .

Could you help me please?

Could you tell me who is in charge of . . .

I'm trying to find out who I should talk to about . . .

What does the person on the other end of the phone know about you immediately? They know you're selling something and they've been instructed to screen you out. Their attitude is "if we're interested, we'll call you." It's now your responsibility to get beyond that barrier. Let's try a totally different approach.

RECEPTIONIST: *Good morning, Holiday Boat Repair.*

SALESPERSON: *Hello, this is Don Bright with Contract Chemicals. I have some information I'd like to forward to the person who makes the decisions about where you purchase shop chemicals. Who should I send this to?*

RECEPTIONIST: *That would probably be Dave Whitt.*

SALESPERSON: *And what is Dave's position please?*

RECEPTIONIST: *He's our shop foreman.*

SALESPERSON: *Would he be available to speak with?*

For now, let's **not** think about what response I'll get once I've asked to speak with Dave Whitt. Instead, let's look at what we've done up to this point.

 What were the key words that were different in this approach?

 We used the terms "send information" and "makes the decisions".

Let's address the use of the term, "send information." We all have tons of information, brochures, literature, catalogs, correspondence, or samples we would love to get in the hands of the decision maker. Is that the reason I mention sending something? I use the term, *send information* because it is non-threatening to the person who answers the phone and ninety-five percent of the time they willingly provide the name. They may even assume the information has been requested.

I'm not advocating you get the name and the position and then run to the mail room with a packet of information that, if sent, will most likely be pitched in the wastebasket. I use the term "send information" only to gain the name. In addition, I said "I would like to send some information," I did not say I was going to send information. Only when I have talked to a decision maker and determined that anything sent would be of mutual interest and benefit, would I ever send anything in the mail.

Let's address the term **"makes the decisions."** What the salesperson said was, *"I have some information I'd like to forward to the person who **makes the decisions**."* This is far more effective than asking for the person *"who takes care of"* or *"does the buying for"* or is *"responsible for."* I want the order maker, not the order placer. In too many cases, the person answering the phone has no idea who the order maker might be.

On the other hand, when I say, *"would make decisions about,"* at least I am getting them to think of someone at a management level rather than someone in a clerical, administrative, or purchasing position. We should always seek to speak with someone as high in the organization as possible. Working down through an organization is easy, working up is not.

Once we have determined the name and position of the decision maker, attempt to get them on the phone. *"Would he be available to speak with?"* Almost said as an afterthought, ask to speak to the person. At this point it's not critical that I get the decision maker on the phone. It would be nice, but not critical because I now have their name and position. I can always call back and ask for them by name or extension. I may even have their direct dial number and I will no longer need to go through the main operator. Using this technique you will get the name and the position of the decision maker 95 percent of the time. If you don't, I guarantee you are not doing it right. You must be assertive but warm to be effective.

The following examples are too passive and will be ineffective more times than not.

- *"Do you think it would be possible to speak with him?"*
- *"Do you think he might have just a few minutes to talk to me?"*
- *"Could you possibly help me?"*
- *"I know he's probably busy but I was wondering if . . ."*

Instead, be more direct or assertive and very warm and friendly. These are examples of asking in a more direct or assertive and **effective** manner while still remaining warm and friendly.

- *"Would he be available now?"*
- *"May I speak with her please?"*
- *"Would you connect me please?"*

A more direct or assertive approach will not be offensive as long as your tone is warm and friendly.

Let's look at that one more time. This time, read aloud playing both roles of receptionist and sales professional yourself. If you have access to a tape recorder, tape the exercise and then play it back. Ask yourself if you were assertive, warm, and confident. Play with it until you are comfortable using your choice of words without changing the technique.

RECEPTIONIST: *Good morning, Holiday Boat Repair.*

SALESPERSON: *Hello, this is Don Bright with Contract Chemicals. I have some information I'd like to forward to the person who makes the deci-*

sions about where you purchase shop chemicals. Who should I send this to?

RECEPTIONIST: *That would probably be Dave Whitt.*

SALESPERSON: *And what is Dave's position please?*

RECEPTIONIST: *He's our shop foreman.*

SALESPERSON: *Would he be available to speak with?*

 What happens when you ask to speak with the decision maker?

 You won't get them, you will get voice mail, or you will get them on the phone.

What happens when the salesperson doesn't connect with the decision maker on the first try? In most cases, you will not get them on the first attempt. Let's look at how a typical call was done in the past.

RECEPTIONIST: *Good morning, Final Touch Incorporated, this is Angie, may I help you?*

SALESPERSON: *Yes, I was wondering if I could talk to the person who takes care of your company's printing needs?*

RECEPTIONIST: *I'm sorry, he's not available at this time. Would you like to leave a message?*

SALESPERSON: *Yes. Please have him call Jill Murray at Cloud's Printing Services. That number is 794-9122.*

What do you think the chances are that Jill Murray will get a return call? Almost zero.

Never, leave a message for a return call when the person you are calling does not know who you are or the purpose of your call. That's playing the old "numbers game." Chances are very remote that you'll receive a return call. If you do, you may be caught totally off guard when they call you back. You need to be in control of the direction of the conversation. That's difficult to do if they catch you off guard. They take a week to return your call and then you can't remember why you left the message, or you are on your way out the door to an important meeting and are forced to terminate the call quickly. This does not make a great first impression.

For example, a couple of years ago, I was in Cincinnati, on a very hot and humid day, consulting and conducting sales training for a client. I had been on my feet for almost nine hours and as I walked across the bubbling hot asphalt parking lot to get to my car, I was dreading the two hour drive home to Columbus in rush hour traffic.

When I got into my steaming car, as is my habit, I used my car phone to call my office voice mail and pick up any messages. One message was from a very polite and professional sounding young man with a charming southern accent. He said he was calling from Alexandria, Virginia and asked that I return his call at my earliest convenience. Because my business originates primarily from referrals, I assumed it was a referral and this person wanted to talk to me about my consulting and training services.

I sat in the hot car with the air conditioner on full blast and called this gentleman only to find out he was a stock broker who wanted to sell me stock. This obviously was not a referral. I was not happy and I let him know it.

"John, I've been working all day and I'm presently calling you long distance on my car phone while stuck in bumper to bumper traffic. The temperature in my car is just now cooling to the low 90's, and you want to talk about selling me stock. I don't think so."

With that, I wished him a good day and hung up.

Who was in control of the direction of that conversation?

 I was in control.

 Who should have been in control of the direction of that conversation?

 The salesperson, however, he chose to abandon control by leaving a message for me to return his call when I did not know who he was or what he wanted.

 What should you do when you don't get them on the first attempt.

A. Be persistent and tenacious.

Among other things, successful sales professionals are persistent and tenacious. Get the direct dial or extension number and then ask when might be the best time to find decision maker available. However, on your first try, don't leave a message for a return call.

Let's look at an example of how a more effective call might go:

RECEPTIONIST: *Good morning, Final Touch Incorporated, this is Angie, how may help you?*

SALESPERSON: *Yes Angie, this is Jill Murray with Clouds Printing Services. I'd like to forward some information to the person who makes the decisions regarding your corporate printing needs. Who would that be please?*

RECEPTIONIST: *That would be Bob Clark.*

SALESPERSON: *And Bob's position?*

RECEPTIONIST: *He's our general manager.*

SALESPERSON: *Would Bob be available to speak with?*

RECEPTIONIST: *No, I'm sorry, he's out of the office today. May I have him return your call?*

SALESPERSON: *No, I'm going to be in and out myself, I'll just try to call him another time. Typically, when is the best time to reach him?*

RECEPTIONIST: *Between 8 and 10 in the mornings. After that he's usually out or in meetings.*

SALESPERSON: *I see. Angie, what is Bob's direct dial or extension number?*

RECEPTIONIST: *His extension is 208.*

SALESPERSON: *Thanks Angie, you've been very helpful. Have a great day.*

Now that you have the name, position and direct dial number, try several times before giving up. If all else fails, you can send information directly to his attention because you now have the specifics instead of lamely sending mail to *"Purchasing Manager."*

If you truly want to be successful in sales, roll out of bed early in the morning and make a few calls over breakfast. Try to catch people sitting at their desk before the receptionist comes to work. Put in a little extra time and stick around the office to make prospecting calls after 6:00 p.m. It's amazing how many decision makers come in early or stay late, and they often answer their own phones when the office is closed.

Q. What can I do if I still can't reach them after several tries.

A. Attempt to speak with someone else who might assist you.

Keep in mind, you are on a fact-finding or "hunting" mission. Any information you can gain about the decision maker's need for your product or service, current supplier or provider, annual budget, time frames, existing problems, etc., is of value when prospecting. While our objective is always to get to the person who calls the shots, sometimes it is just not possible without assistance.

Here are some guidelines when attempting to contact the presumed decision maker:

- First try, don't leave a message.
- Second try, don't leave a message.
- Third try, don't leave a message. The assumption is that your tries are at different times and days.
- After the third try, ask to speak with a secretary, assistant, co-worker, or someone who works closely with the decision maker.

Let's look at how that call might go:

RECEPTIONIST: *I'm sorry, Tom is out of the office today. Would you like his voice mail?*

SALESPERSON: *Thank you, but if possible, I would really like to speak to someone else. I've tried several times to reach Tom but we just can't seem to connect. Does Tom have a secretary or assistant, someone he works closely with regarding corporate travel needs that I might speak with in his absence?*

RECEPTIONIST: *That would be Nancy Owens. She takes care of scheduling service and new installations. Just a moment and I'll see if she's available.*

SALESPERSON: *Thank you. (call is being transferred to Nancy)*

ASSISTANT: *Hello, this is Nancy.*

SALESPERSON: *Hello Nancy, this is Lee Brown with Broner's Corporate Travel. Nancy, I was told that Tom is the person that makes the decisions regarding corporate travel services for your company. Is that true?*

ASSISTANT: *Yes, but he's not in the office today.*

SALESPERSON: *Yes, I knew that, but I was hoping you might be able to help me. Broner's is very interested in having the opportunity to do business with your company and I've been attempting to reach Tom, but so far, we've just not been able to connect. Nancy, could you suggest what would be the best way for me to proceed?*

ASSISTANT: *Well, I doubt he will be interested in talking to you until later this year. He's currently in the middle of a big project with some tight deadlines. In fact, he'll be out of the office most of the next 90 days. Tom reviews contracts the last quarter of the year and if you want to send in some information . . .*

That call resulted in some very useful information. Rather than asking, *"How do I reach Tom?,"* We've put the emphasis on *"How would you suggest I proceed,"* which aids in gaining respect and co-operation. Most secretaries, assistants, and support staff want to help and will help when the person making inquiries is honest, up front, and not demanding.

When information gained from someone other than the decision maker clearly indicates there is little or no opportunity for doing business with a company, that's a real plus. In sales, the next best thing to a firm yes is a firm no. Everything in between is often a big waste of time. Don't ever underestimate the value of fact-finding with someone other than the decision maker. The key is showing respect for the other person's position and being honest from the first point of contact.

If this approach still does not get you through to the decision maker, use your newly acquired information to draft a knowledgeable letter directed to their attention. The letter can serve as your first step towards gaining interest and attention.

Remember, when making fact-finding, qualifying prospecting calls, get the name and the position before ever asking to speak with anyone.

 What about voice mail?

 Don't be too quick to leave a message.

A few years ago, voice mail was only found in larger corporations. Today it's completely different. Even small businesses have chosen to install voice mail systems. This does not mean you will never be able to speak with the decision maker. It just means it may take more effort on your part. Be persistent and tenacious. Don't be too quick to leave a message on the first few attempts.

Here are a few additional don'ts when telephone prospecting and leaving voice mail messages.

■ Don't page anyone to come to the phone when you are prospecting or call them on their car phone.

Unless you have something that is guaranteed to cure cancer, eliminate rush hour traffic, or keep interest rates at below 2 percent for business loans, don't page prospective customers to come to the phone. Don't ask for them to be paged and don't use their pager numbers, even if they leave that option on a voice mail message.

Pagers and car phones are for important calls, important to the decision maker, not the salesperson. If you pursue them on their pager or car phone, 95 percent of the time, you will risk beginning the relationship on the wrong foot.

■ Don't leave a voice mail infomercial or commercial or a message that begins with, "Have I got a deal for you!"

Do not start out with:

"I wanted to take just a minute to tell you about our new software program that can literally save hundreds of hours and thousands of dollars in payroll expenses. We've just developed this software and we have a very small quantity available to select clients and I was positive you would . . ."

Voice mail messages should never be "dog and pony shows." They should be done in good taste and in a manner that sends a message to the decision maker that you are an honest, up-front professional with integrity and you are worthy of consideration. Remember to **woo** your prospect. Don't kiss on the first date.

■ Don't use trickery or deceptive tactics.

I once heard about a sales trainer who taught sales people to call business decision makers on the pretext they had found their business card on their desk and did not know why it was there. The call went something like this:

"Hello John, this is Mary Smith with XYZ Company. I have your business card on my desk and for the life of me, I'm not sure why. Was I supposed to call you about something?"

Today, techniques like this would and should be an embarrassment to any true sales professional.

In another instance, I was told about a sales manager teaching his staff to leave incomplete voice mail messages to create a sense of urgency or curiosity. Those calls went like this:

"Hi Wendy, this is Dyana Holmes with ABC Enterprises, 614-000-1111 ext: 007. I need to speak with you about the . . ." and then the sound of the dial tone.

This was supposed to make the prospect curious enough to call back to find out the rest of the message. Quite frankly, if that happened to me, I would be worried my voice mail was in need of technical attention. Generally, calls like this aggravate a decision maker and do little to establish rapport or respect. The best rule of thumb is to be honest. Leave a truthful voice mail message that creates a professional image of the salesperson.

 What are some "do's" in leaving good, professional voice mail message.

 Always be honest, clear and brief.

Leave a very clear message that identifies..

■ Who you are.
■ Why you are calling.
■ What you want.

Let's look at how a more effective call might go.

"Good morning Bob, this is Allison Cook with Today's Employment Service. 794-0134. Bob, I understand you're the person that makes the decisions about temporary employment needs at your company, and Today's is very interested in having the opportunity to do business with your firm. Would you please give me a call when it's convenient and let me

---

know what would be the best way for us to proceed. Again, my name is Allison Cook with Today's Employment Service. 794-0134. Thank you, Bob, and have a great day.

Does Bob know why she's calling? Yes! Is there any doubt in his mind? No! She made it very clear. *"We're interested in having the opportunity to do business with your firm and what do we need to do to make that happen?"* She will have spoken slowly enough and clearly enough that the listener was able to understand her name, first and last, company name, and the telephone number. The sales person even repeated that information. Will Bob run to the phone and call her right back? Probably not, but his first impression of this salesperson is that she is friendly, honest, and a professional. That's a great start on building a new account. If the decision maker never returns her call, but she is able to get him on the phone at a later date, he may remember her message and extend to her the same honesty and openness. Also, if I choose to send information by mail, I may now have a better chance that it will be opened and read. So far, we've discussed the importance of being honest. Now, let's deal with the importance of being clear.

 Do I need to give both my first and last name?

 It's a personal preference.

If you choose to use your complete name, make sure it sounds as if you have two names, not one long one. For example, if I say:

"Hello, this is WinnieAry,"

without a distinct break between each name, the person retrieving the message may hear this as one name, not two. Take a minute and say your own name out loud using both first and last. Run them together as I did.

Now, say it again with a clear and distinct break between the two names. For example:

"Hello, this is Winnie (slight pause) Ary, with Ary Group Inc."

Can you hear the difference?

Experts tell us that we speak at 140 to 160 words per minute on the average and think at 400 to 600 words per minute. When I say my name, company name, my product or service name, telephone number, etc. and the party I'm speaking to doesn't understand one or more words, I risk losing their attention. They may begin thinking about what I just said and no longer be listening to what I'm saying.

Another reminder, because we are so familiar with our own names and telephone numbers, it is tempting to rush through them. Say them both clearly and slowly enough for someone to write it down. Then repeat it so they can verify accuracy without the need to replay the message. Clarity is critical in telephone communication because there isn't body language or written material to support what was just said.

As important as honesty and clarity is to the voice mail message, so is being brief.

> The telephone is not a tool to make an appointment . . .
> it *is* an appointment.

In this case, it is your first appointment and everyone knows you never get a second chance to make a first impression. Keep your message brief and to the point, don't leave messages that run more than 45 to 60 seconds when you are attempting to build rapport with a prospective client, avoid infomercials and commercials, and stick to the purpose of the call.

 **KEY POINTS**

- **"Send information"** is less threatening than "may I speak with" and will generate more positive results.

- Using the phrase "makes the decisions" is more effective than "takes care of, in charge of, or does the purchasing of." **"Makes decisions"** will get you to the management level more often.

- Don't leave messages for return calls when they don't know who you are or what you want.

- Ask for the position. *"And his position, please?"* Be assertive but warm.

- Once you have the name and position, almost as an afterthought, ask to speak with them. *"Is she available?"* Be assertive but warm.

- If, after several attempts, you are unable to make contact with the decision maker, ask to speak with an assistant.

- If you must leave a voice mail message, make it a good one. Most important, be honest, clear, and brief.

*There Is
No Such Thing
as a
Born Salesperson.
Selling Is
Learned Behavior!*

Winnie Ary

Verify Decision Maker and Ask for the Business

3

We've addressed the importance of getting the name and position of the decision maker. We've also addressed options when we have not initially reached them by phone. Knowing we must eventually make contact in order to begin the selling process, let's now address what to do when we finally reach our presumed decision maker.

Getting our decision maker on the phone can be a time consuming task that often entails numerous telephone attempts, correspondence, and conversations with assistants, secretaries or other personnel. However, we finally connect. What happens now? Do you feel scared? Nervous? Caught off guard?

I love the story about Butch, the dog that chased every car that dared drive through his neighborhood. Up to the day old Butch died, everyone in the neighborhood made bets on what the dog would do it he ever caught one of the cars. He never did, so I guess we'll never know.

Many sales professionals can relate chasing down decision makers to Butch's chasing down the cars. What do we do when we finally catch them?

Most salespeople have been trained to start presenting the moment they make contact with the presumed decision maker. They attempt to say everything about who they are and what they have to offer in one big breath.

Let's look at an example of what we mean.

SALESPERSON: *"Hello Joe, my name is Clara Smith with O'Toole's Catering. I'm calling to see if you would allow me the opportunity to meet with you to discuss your corporate catering needs. I promise not to take more than 20 minutes of your time, I know people in your position get very busy.*

We're family owned and operated and we've been in business for almost 25 years in this area. In addition to having a full service restaurant and banquet room we offer a variety of on site catering services that include business luncheons, company picnics, holiday parties, open house and things of that nature. Our menu is very extensive and we can cater anything from box luncheons to formal sit down dinners.

I'll be calling on businesses in your area next week and I was hoping I could schedule an appointment for us to get acquainted and discuss some of the ways we might be of service to your company. I'm wide open on next Tuesday or Thursday in the mornings but if you would prefer afternoon I would be available . . ."

I call this the "burp gun" approach. Just suck in a deep breath and let it all out in one, big burp!

Business professionals get very turned off by the "burp gun" approach and even more by being asked for an appointment before they have expressed any interest. Remember, if they were already interested, they would have called you.

 Why do sales people use the "burp gun" approach?

 The number one reason is fear of rejection.

We say to ourselves, "I don't want to hear no or go away." We think that if we throw everything we have to offer in one hard toss, something is going to hit the mark. We hope that something we say will surely strike a hot button and they'll grant an appointment or begin showing interest in our product or service. The reality is, that very rarely happens.

 Why doesn't the "burp gun" approach work?

 The prospective customer is generally not listening.

We think so much faster than we speak so it's easy for the person you are addressing to tune you out if they are not interested in hearing what you have to say. Instead of listening they are thinking of excuses or reasons to say no or to cut you off and terminate the call. In essence, you have not gained their attention.

 Why is the "burp gun" technique still encouraged by sales managers and many sales trainers?

 Most of them still believe that getting a face to face appointment is all that matters, so "push hard and get in," or as we discussed earlier in this book, "kiss on the first date."

Over the years, I've seen hundreds of scripts prepared by managers and trainers that dictate what the salesperson is to say when they get a prospective customer on the phone. Ninety nine percent of the scripts were burp gun presentations focused on one thing, get an appointment in order to pitch your product or service.

 If the "burp gun" approach does not work, what can we do to avoid hearing no or facing rejection?

 Absolutely nothing, nor should we want to do anything to avoid a negative response or an objection.

We've all heard the saying, "The selling begins when the customer says no!" Well it's true. What do we expect the prospective client to say when we call and ask for an appointment or pitch a product or service? *"Oh, I'm so glad you called, come on over?"* We can't avoid the objection, so learn to embrace it and respond effectively .

 What should we say when we make telephone contact with the prospect for the first time?

 As little as necessary to verify we are speaking to the appropriate decision maker.

For example:

PROSPECT: *This is Mark.*

SALESPERSON: *Good morning Mark, this is Pat Wilson with HRL Equipment. Mark, I was given your name as the person who makes the decisions about equipment rentals for construction projects. Is that true?*

Now at this point you can expect to get a yes, no, or some variation as an answer. Example:

"Yes, but I've got all I need at this time."

Now, concentrate on what **you** have just said and **how** you said it, instead of Mark's response.

Key points when verifying the decision maker.

1. **Begin with a strong, confident opening.** You have about 15 to 20 seconds to make a positive first impression and gain attention. This is your telephone **"handshake"** and we all know how important a good firm handshake is in making a positive first impression.

Get rid of terms like, "you guys, ya know, and yeah." You can't talk to a 40 or 50-year-old decision maker like you're having a beer and pizza with your buddies on Friday night and get him to take you seriously on the phone. Business people will not take you seriously, regardless of how good you might be face to face. If you sound unprofessional on the phone, you will lose credibility. You must make the effort to sound mature, polished and professional. Use professional and industry—specific terms as much as possible. In addition try standing up when you are on the phone. It is a great help in projecting and sounding more confident.

Grammar, diction, energy level, and confidence are all important to gaining interest and attention. When you do not have body language and eye contact to help overcome weaknesses in how you speak, you must make sure your communication skills are equal to the task at hand.

2. **Get on a first name basis.** Most Americans do business on a first name basis. Today, those who are still using Mr. or Mrs. in business dealings are clearly in the minority. These addresses are generally restricted to written correspondence.

Business cards reflect first names and often our nicknames. William becomes "Bill" in parenthesis and Catherine may show her name as " Kate." We answer our phones and leave voice mail messages with our first name. What happens when Marie, a twenty-nine-year-old sales professional, contacts Jack Jones, a fifty-year-old decision maker, and says,

Good Morning **Mr. Jones,** *my name is* **Marie** *and I represent the Ace Corporation . . .*

Who is now in control? Where has Marie positioned herself in the pecking order? Does she view herself as subservient to Jack? It certainly sounds like she does. That is not an acceptable position for today's consultative sales professional.

Get on a first name basis and don't ask permission. Just do it. It will be rare that you will be wrong in doing so. When you don't you have positioned yourself as less than equal. In consultative, relationship selling, less than equal is anything but favorable.

There are some exceptions. Use professional titles such as Dr., General, Reverend, etc. When addressing business professionals from other countries you are much safer using Mr. and Mrs. when beginning a relationship. European and Asian business culture is more formal than ours.

3. **Finish verifying the decision maker with a question.** For example:

"Allen, I was told you are the person who makes the decisions about where your company purchases office supplies. Is that true?" or, "Is that correct?" or, "Is my information accurate?"

You direct the conversation when you finish the verification with a question. They will direct where the conversation goes if you do not. Most people will not lie and say they are the decision maker when they are not.

---

4. Back out if you have the wrong person. Don't take no from a person who can't say yes.

You really want to get the person who makes decisions. If you allow the conversation to continue too long when you have the wrong person, you may find yourself permanently shut out. Here's an example of how to back out gracefully.

SALESPERSON: *Hello Barry, this is Jessica Thomas with Johnson Rentals. Barry, I was told you make the decisions regarding light equipment rentals for the construction crews. Is my information correct?*

PROSPECT: *No it's not. I only approve the invoices for payment and make sure we apply the costs to the right project.*

SALESPERSON: *I'm sorry, I was given the wrong information. Barry, who should I be speaking with regarding light equipment rental?*

Don't encourage extraneous conversation at this point. Politely attempt to get the appropriate name and move on. If you are not able to reach the true decision maker, you can always go back to this person for additional information. Initially, it is always a plus to make contact with the right person. We said it earlier, it's easier to work down in the organization than to start at the bottom and try to work up.

On occasions we'll run into multiple decision maker situations. When this happens just continue forward. If you've made contact with one of the people involved with making decisions, treat them as if they had full authority. Don't probe to determine which of the group is "top dog". You may risk offending the person, particularly if everyone thinks they hold that position. At this point, we are not attempting to close a sale. We are prospecting to determine potential for business and get our foot in the door. Once in, determining which of the "group" carries the most clout is generally not difficult. For now, focus on how to get in.

 What happens after we verify the decision maker?

 Ask for the business.

This may be one of the most difficult techniques to master as you work to develop your telephone prospecting and selling skills. There are salespeople who go their entire careers and never become comfortable or competent at asking for the business.

How can you be successful in sales if you can't ask for the business? Let's look at some examples of "asking for the business."

Joe, I'm calling because our company would love the opportunity to do business with your firm. What's the best way for us to proceed to make that happen?

United Plus provides computer training and needs analysis. Mary, I was hoping you could tell me how we could become the company you contact when those needs arise?

Tom, we feel that our business banking services fit well with companies similar to your own in size and business type. How could we go about earning your business?

Don't hint, suggest or beg. Ask for the business. We are not calling to see if we can help them out or to see if they need anything. We're calling to ask for the business. Is that wrong? If you think it is then I suggest you close this book right now and spend your time putting together a resume targeted to a non-sales position. Would you attempt to run a business with sales people who thought asking for the business was wrong?

Let's look at how this flows when we put it all together:

PROSPECT: *This is Mark.*

SALESPERSON: *Good morning Mark, this is Pat Wilson with HRL Equipment. Mark, I was given your name as the person who makes the decisions about equipment rentals for your company's construction projects. Is that true?*

PROSPECT: *Yes, but right now all projects are well covered.*

SALESPERSON: *I understand and I appreciate your honesty. Mark, we'd like the opportunity to earn your equipment rental business. How could we position ourselves for consideration on your next project?*

Was the salesperson pushy, obnoxious, high-pressure? Not at all. How do you think the prospective customer feels about a salesperson who calls and (a) gets to the point and (b) tells the truth about why they are calling? I'll be greatly surprised if you don't find the results extremely positive and rewarding.

Don't be concerned with the response you will get when you ask for the business. We'll cover that in detail in our next chapter. For now, here are key points to remember when asking for the business.

1. **Assume the need.** Don't talk yourself out of making the call because you're not sure they use the product or service you sell. If you find out they are not a good prospect, turn it into a public relations or "PR" call. Example:

SALESPERSON: *United Plus provides temporary employee services. Mary, I was hoping you could tell me how we could become the company you would contact when those needs arise?*

PROSPECT: *Katie, I'll be honest. I'll bet we have not used a temporary service more than 3 or 4 times in the last 5 years, and It was generally when we took inventory and we've got that all on computer now.*

SALESPERSON: *Well I appreciate your taking the time to speak with me today and Mary, if your situation ever changes, I hope you'll let us know.*

Our salesperson, Katie, determined the potential for business was too little to justify further effort and choose to turn this into a PR call, not wasting anyone's time. She can always place this account in her contact management program or follow-up file and call again in 6 to 12 months to see if anything has changed. For now, there is no reason to continue dialog. No damage was done as a result of asking for the business.

2. **State the purpose of the call.** Don't lie, hint or skirt the issue. Tell the truth. Here are some examples of ineffective ways to ask for the business.

I was just calling to see if you might be interested in hearing about a special we have going on at this time.

(Too passive, almost apologetic)

Would it be possible to take a minute of your time and ask a few questions. I just wanted to see if there might be some areas we could be of service.

(We're begging and setting ourselves up for a no!)

I was calling to see if you would like to receive some information about our company and the products we offer?

(Weak and ineffective. It's not likely the prospective customer will take the salesperson seriously.)

3. Listen for the response. Don't say a word. Don't even breathe heavily. Once you have asked for the business, say nothing. Give them an opportunity to hit you with the first point of resistance, the first objection, or the first "no". This is the time for them to hit you with the very thing you have been avoiding. Learning to confidently and competently ask for the business will open doors for you and expose opportunities you never knew were there.

Here are a few competent, skillful examples:

a. You are currently doing business in one division or department of a large company but not another. Pick up the phone, call the other division and ask for the business.

SALESPERSON: *Martha, I understand from James Wirth that you take care of temporary employment for the warehouse facility. We're currently working with him at the corporate office and we'd like to provide the same service for the warehouse. What would be your requirements for us to have that opportunity?*

b. Collect business cards while attending a business function and call the next week and ask for the business. Don't worry about the fact that the person you met and whose card you possess works in customer service and you need to get to the person making decisions on client appreciation gifts and other corporate gift giving.

SALESPERSON: *John, how are you, this is Cindy with Corporate Incentives. We met last week at the Chamber meeting. John, I was hoping you could help me. I'm very interested in doing business with your company with regard to any corporate gift giving they do.*

I was hoping you might suggest a way for me to get my foot in the door?

   c. You read in the paper that a company in another city is opening a branch office in your area in about 6 months and you want to address their business equipment needs. Call, ask for the business, and incorporate in your conversation the information (the hook) you read in the paper.

SALESPERSON: *Good morning, Richard. My name is Dana Robbins and I'm an account executive with Greenbriar Business Machines. I recently read in our local business publication you're starting a branch office in our area. I wanted to make contact with you to determine how we could position ourselves to handle your office equipment needs. What would be the first step for that to be a possibility?*

   d. You met someone at a social event who works for a company that could be a great prospect for business. It would not have been appropriate to discuss business that evening. It's been a few days and you now wish to make contact.

SALESPERSON: *Sandra, Melissa Springer. We met at the church bazaar last week. (After the pleasantries are exchanged, get to the point.) Sandra I'll be brief, I know you're at work. I'm an account representative with T & L Accounting and we'd really like to work with your company. Could you suggest who would be the right person for me to contact?*

Becoming confident and competent in asking for the business takes time and practice. However, when it comes to prospecting for business it can be the single most important skill you master. Here are a few more tips to aid in that process.

- Avoid statements like "And, how are you today?" At least not the first time you speak to a prospective client. It reeks of "Tillie Telemarketer."

- Speak in a warm but assertive manner. If you sound apologetic, nothing you say will have much impact. See the call as an opportunity, not an interruption. That must be clearly heard in the tone of your voice.

- On a first contact, don't ask "Is this a good time or, do you have a minute." Until you have developed at least some rapport, 99 percent of the time, the prospect will use that opportunity to just get rid of you. It's ok not to ask if they have a minute. If you sense you've caught them at a bad time or they tell you it's a bad time, then reschedule the call. (We'll address that in Chapter Four.) Continuing dialog when you know the timing is not good for the prospect is pushy and not professional. On the other hand, If they don't mention bad timing, press on.

Develop your own style for :

determining the decision maker
verifying decision maker
asking for the business

If you don't presently own a tape recorder, go buy one. It will be one of the best investments you'll ever make to aid in developing professional selling skills. Record a make believe call where you attempt to determine the name and position of the decision maker through asking for the business. Play both roles yourself unless you have a friend or family member willing to assist. Say it over and over into the tape recorder until it sounds right, feels good, and you're confident it will be effective. Then, write down word for word, exactly what you said. Write your script from what you said, not the other way around. Otherwise, it may sound "canned" or staged. Say what is comfortable for you to say, making sure you use the techniques presented in the book. This is the example we gave in chapter two.

SALESPERSON: *Hello, this is Don Bright with Contract Chemicals. I have some information I'd like to forward to the person who makes the decisions about where you purchase shop chemicals. Who should I send this to?*

Use the same techniques while adding your own communication style and it will sound altogether different. Example:

SALESPERSON: *Good morning, my name is Don Bright and I'm with Contract Chemicals. I'm attempting to send an information packet to the individual making decisions about chemicals that are purchased for the shop. Who would be the person in charge of those decisions?*

See the difference? Same technique, different communication style. Here is one more example to assist you as you begin your exercise.

RECEPTIONIST: *Good Afternoon, Lynette Publishing. How may I help you?*

SALESPERSON: *Good afternoon, this is Clark Jacobs with Metro Office Environments here in Columbus. I have some information I'd like to send to the person who makes decisions about your office furniture needs. Who would that be please?*

RECEPTIONIST: *That would be Jamie Wooster.*

SALESPERSON: *And what is Jamie's position please?*

RECEPTIONIST: *She's the Vice President of Finance and General Manager.*

SALESPERSON: *By chance would she be available to speak with?*

RECEPTIONIST: *I'll see if I can connect you.*

PROSPECT: *This is Jamie.*

SALESPERSON: *Hello Jamie, my name is Clark Jacobs with Metro Office Environments. Jamie, I was told you're the person who makes decisions about office furniture needs at Lynette Publishing. Is that correct?*

JAMIE: *Yes.*

SALESPERSON: *Great. Well, Jamie, I'm calling today because Metro is considered one of the best office furniture dealers in the country and we would really like to do business with Lynette Publishing. Could you tell me how we could earn that opportunity?*

Start practicing.

KEY POINTS FOR CHAPTER THREE

■ Verify you are speaking with the decision maker rather than asking. Asking and verifying are not the same thing.

■ Always finish verifying with a question: "Is that true?" "Is that correct?"

■ Prepare to back out if you are not speaking with the true decision maker.

■ Get on a first name basis except in extenuating circumstances.

■ Always assume there is a need for your product/service.

■ Ask for the business. No hinting, suggesting or begging.

■ After asking for the business, be silent and wait for a response.

■ Don't be a "burp gun" . . . it's not professional.

Profit Is Not a Luxury. It's a Necessity.

Winnie Ary

Listening and Addressing Resistance

4

If you practiced you should now be fairly comfortable with how to determine, reach, and verify you have your decision maker, and ask for the business. What happens next?

Once we have asked for their business and stopped talking, we should expect a positive response, right? Something like, "Wow, I can't believe your timing, come on over." While there is something to be said for timing, it will be rare you will ever hear such a positive greeting when making cold calls.

 Q. What will we typically hear when we ask for the business?

 A. Exactly what we all hope to avoid, the first point of resistance, an objection.

At this point in a cold call, the decision maker is generally not interested in talking to you. If they were, they would have called you. Their objective is to get rid of you, to make you go away. Some are more polite than others, but they still are saying the same thing.

What you are likely to hear is one or more of the following points of resistance:

1. Send me some information in the mail and I'll look it over.
2. We're happy with who we're currently doing business with.
3. I'm too busy to talk to you right now.
4. We're really not interested.
5. We had a bad experience with your company and we don't want to do business with you again.
6. We don't have any money at this time.
7. You're too late, we just bought.
8. You're too early, we're not ready to buy.
9. I'm not familiar with your company.
10. We don't need anything right now.
11. You would have to give us a better price.
12. My brother-in-law is in the business and we buy everything at cost.

Sales professionals everywhere regularly hear one or more of those same responses when prospecting for new business.

Statistics indicate that ninety percent of those who **don't succeed in sales** fail because of their inability to effectively address the first objection. To many, addressing that first objection or point of resistance can be so terrifying they refuse to prospect.

"Look, I'm doing business with someone else and I see no reason to change,"

is often more frightening to hear than the fear of losing their job.

 Why are we so afraid of the first point of resistance when cold calling by telephone?

 Two reasons.

First, we've never had to prospect for new business. Second, most have had little or no training in *how* to effectively respond. Let's address never having the need to prospect.

Early in my consulting career, one of my clients was struggling with how to develop new business. They sold a high priced product that for a number of years, had been in big demand. During the good years, it was not uncommon for the company to receive calls almost daily from prospective clients wanting to schedule appointments with sales representatives. Orders for product were frequently received by mail, totally unsolicited. A salesperson with even reasonably good product knowledge made an upper six-figure income without the need to prospect. Some years later, however, the product became viewed almost as a commodity, competition was fierce, and profit margins were declining. Now, for the first time, the company needed to aggressively prospect for new accounts. The sales staff on the other hand, was waiting for the phone to ring or for the company to **assign** them a new account. Some were hoping other sales people would be fired or retire so they could **inherit** their accounts. In some cases the resistance to prospecting can be so intense it becomes necessary to dismiss the salesperson. As painful as it was to accept, this is exactly what my client was forced to do.

How many companies do you know where the top salesperson is #1 because they held on the longest and acquired the best accounts? Unfortunately, I've seen companies go bankrupt because seasoned, knowledgeable sales people refused to master the skills necessary to prospect for business and management either did not recognize or address the source of the problem.

Let's look at how a few of the most frequently heard objections are commonly addressed in a totally **ineffective** manner.

PROSPECT: *Send me some information in the mail and I'll look it over.*

SALESPERSON: *I'll do that and maybe I can call back in a week or two and see if you have any questions. Now let me verify that address. I show 1322 E. Main Street . . .*

Why is this response so ineffective? The decision maker said, "go away," and the sales person said, in so many words, "OK." This was a polite, accommodating call. It was also worthless. Here is another example:

PROSPECT: *We're currently doing business with so and so and we're happy.*

SALESPERSON: *I'm familiar with so and so and they are a good company, but I'm confident that if I could show you how our product could save you . . .*

While I agree we should never make negative remarks about the competition, I'm not going to sing their praises. This sales person said *"they are a good company."* That statement only validated that the prospective customer had made a wise choice in selecting that vendor. However, worse than singing the competitors praises, the salesperson went into a "sales pitch" when confronted with the objection. I call this the "but, but, but" response. The sales person was just not listening. Another example:

PROSPECT: *You would have to give us a better price.*

SALESPERSON: *Well, where do we need to be?*

I call this the "give it away response." This approach may sometimes gain you the sale, but it's very dangerous. If the only thing that counts is presenting the lowest price, your company may not need sales people. They can hire someone for a small hourly fee to sit on the phone all day and quote the lowest price. As sales professionals, we truly put ourselves at risk when we lead with price. Profit is not a luxury, it's a necessity. Last but not least, my favorite:

PROSPECT:	*We don't need anything right now.*
SALESPERSON:	*Well, please keep us in mind if anything changes.*

Most sales professionals can recall having made the statement, "keep us in mind." While rarely effective, it's often the standard response used by salespeople when confronted with an objection they are not trained or confident in addressing.

 How can we avoid objections or customer resistance?

 You can't and you shouldn't. Embrace the resistance, don't run from it.

Selling is learned behavior. We will hear many of the same questions, objections, and concerns in any business. It's knowing what to do and when to do it that separates the skilled sales professional from the one who struggles.

Let's focus on some more effective ways to address the first objection or "brush off." Look for the common denominators in each of these examples.

PROSPECT:	*Send me some information in the mail and I'll look it over.*
SALESPERSON:	*I'll be happy to send you a catalog and my business card. Joe, could I first ask where you are currently purchasing your machine fasteners?*

In a sense, the prospective customer had said, "go away." The salesperson, however, responded with a question.

Here is another example of the prospective customer resisting the salesperson:

PROSPECT: *We're currently doing business with so and so and we're happy.*

SALESPERSON: *I understand. John, what would have to happen for you to at least consider looking at an alternative service?*

Once again, the salesperson addressed the resistance with a question.

Looking at another scenario:

PROSPECT: *You would have to give us a better price.*

SALESPERSON: *Eric, let's assume for just a moment we could give you prices as good or better than your are currently getting. What other issues are important to you when selecting a supplier?*

In this instance the salesperson did not give in to the challenge presented by the prospective customer, instead he addressed it by asking a question.

Our last example:

PROSPECT: *We don't need anything right now.*

SALESPERSON: *Rene, what can we do to position ourselves so that when you are ready to order, we could be considered?*

In every example the salesperson demonstrated three key competencies that are necessary in effective telephone prospecting.

1. **The salesperson clearly listened.**
2. **The salesperson was persistent but not pushy.**
3. **The salesperson made a smooth transition from listening, to a question.**

While this technique won't always lead to an appointment or a sale on a first attempt, it works far more often than giving up or becoming defensive. In addition, it's generally much less difficult getting the decision maker on the phone a second time. When we give up too easily or become defensive the decision maker may not take you seriously or simply just choose to avoid you. On the other hand, if you listen to what the prospect has just said and respond with an appropriate question, there is a good chance you may turn the entire call around and begin having a quality conversation. If you can get the prospect to talk, rapport and interest may begin to develop.

 Is there only one possible response for each point of resistance?

 Absolutely not. There can be as many as you choose.

It's not memorizing the responses that makes this work. It's learning the technique. It's mastering the competency.

Let's look at one commonly heard objection addressed five different ways.

PROSPECT:	*Send me some information in the mail and I'll look it over.*
SALESPERSON:	*I'll be happy to send you a catalog and my business card. Joe, may I ask where you are currently purchasing your chemicals?*

or,

PROSPECT:	*Send me some information in the mail and I'll look it over.*
SALESPERSON:	*No problem. Jim, how many components are you using on a quarterly basis?*

PROSPECT: *Send me some information in the mail and I'll look it over.*

SALESPERSON: *I'll get that in today's mail. Erin, would you share with me a little about how you are currently handling your heavy equipment repairs?*

or,

PROSPECT: *Send me some information in the mail and I'll look it over.*

SALESPERSON: *I'll do that. Karen, what type of projects do you generally target in your business?*

or,

PROSPECT: *Send me some information in the mail and I'll look it over.*

SALESPERSON: *Certainly, but what do you look for in selecting the distributors you'll use in each of your territories, Daren?*

Making a smooth transition from listening to a question is very important. Asking the question in an assertive but warm and friendly manner is equally important. Firing off questions in rapid succession or sounding like the chief interrogator for the police department won't get you positive results. Ask questions in a conversational, focused and non threatening manner. When making cold calls, the prospect is rarely interested in what information we might send. They tell us to send something in the mail in an attempt to terminate an unsolicited sales call. It's a way to get rid of what they initially perceive is an "interruption." We play odds that are not in our favor when we assume they may become interested once it's received. In reality, our literature will probably end up in the waste basket, and the prospect will never remember telling us to send it in the first place. Instead, seize the opportunity to turn the call around and attempt to gain the prospects interest and attention.

This is not the end. This is the beginning. At this point, we have the best opportunity to turn a telephone call into a telephone appointment. Remember, what we have said from the beginning, "The telephone is not a tool to make an appointment . . . it *is* an appointment."

After asking for the business, listening and responding appropriately to the first objection is critical to moving forward. This is where we have our best opportunity to position ourselves to begin the fact-finding and qualifying part of prospecting.

Expect that decision makers will not be interested when you call and be prepared to deal with that effectively. This means practice, taking risk, and developing your skill. Don't give up when you hear that first "go away."

My husband, Earl, and I had a dog named Lovie, who was like our child for over 14 years. When she passed away, we missed her terribly but found great comfort in remembering the fun we had with her over the years. One evening, we were talking about what happened the night she was first introduced to our boat. I could not help but connect that particular incident to sales people.

We had purchased our first boat and it was docked at a marina on Lake Erie in Port Clinton, Ohio. After driving two and a half hours from our home in Westerville, we finally arrived at the boat. It was early April, dark, and cold and our first night on our new boat. It took several trips to unload, so we decided to leave Lovie in the car until we were finished. Finally, it was time to take her down the dock and onto the boat.

Lovie was so devoted to Earl that we never needed a leash. She followed him everywhere he went with undying devotion and blind trust. Earl is over six feet tall with very long legs and Lovie was a six pound dog with little short legs. Just as Earl lifted his leg over the side of the boat, Lovie leaped to join him. She did not leap high enough or hard enough, falling into about 20 feet of ice cold water. Almost as quickly as she hit the water, her head popped up and she was climbing the rocks to get out of the water. She let us know she was not happy, pouting for two days refusing to eat or drink.

We boated for seven years and never once without Lovie. Actually, in many ways she became a better boater than I did. However, for seven years when we reached the beginning of the walkway to the dock, she plopped her bottom on the ground. She had to be carried to and from the boat. Lovie had once taken a risk, and it had been a painful experience. She was never willing to take that risk again.

Many sales professionals have done the same thing. They tried it once and it did not work so they gave up. Many of us are expecting someone to carry us to the account or to the sale because we don't want to do the prospecting.

Key Points for Chapter Four

■ Listen and smoothly transition to a question.

■ There are many different ways to respond to the same objection.

■ Effectively addressing the first objection is where we have the best opportunity to turn a telephone sales call into a telephone appointment.

■ Selling is learned behavior. PRACTICE!

■ Remember: Responding effectively to the first objection is not the end, it's the beginning.

It's Our Job to Make to Make Them Thirsty.

Winnie Ary

Fact-Finding
and Qualifying

5

 Once we've made the transition from listening to a question, where do we go next?

 Fact-finding and qualifying.

People buy for two primary reasons. They trust us and they feel we know and understand their needs. The most effective way to develop trust and understanding when telephone prospecting is to ask questions. Remember the "wooing" process we mentioned in Chapter Three. The kiss without the "wooing" may not be well received. It's the same in sales, when we attempt to push for an appointment or push our product or service too soon the prospect may feel threatened, uncomfortable, angry and even offended.

Effective fact-finding and qualifying focuses on the prospect's concerns, business, and needs. This is critical to developing rapport, trust, understanding and interest.

 Should I have a list of questions to ask, prepared in advance, before making cold calls?

Yes and No. It can be risky if we don't know what we're doing.

Let's look at the pro's and con's of using a prepared list of questions or forms when fact-finding and qualifying.

Assume for this exercise we sell office furniture to businesses. For cold calling purposes, a fact finding and qualifying list of questions might look like this:

1. Current vendor
2. Number of office staff
3. Additional locations
4. Nature of business
5. Annual budget
6. Primary interest
And so on . . .

The questions are pretty straight forward, but when fact finding, if we are not focused on the prospect's needs, they may feel as if they are being interrogated.

In other instances a salesperson or even a sales manager, may choose to prepare a list of questions to be read exactly as written. That list might look like this:

1. *Who do you usually buy furniture from?*
2. *How many office staff do you have in your company?*
3. *Is this your only location?*
4. *What is it that your company does?*
5. *Do you have a budget for office furniture?*
6. *What is your primary concern when purchasing office furniture?*
And so on . . .

Either way, our tendency is to read question one because it's first, question two because it's next, and so on. At best, prepared questions or forms when fact-finding and qualifying without having mastered the technique is risky.

Look at an example of what can happen when a salesperson is focused on their list of questions or their own agenda and not listening to what is being said by the prospect.

SALESPERSON: *Stacy, Overbrook is very interested in doing business with your company. Could you tell me how we might make that happen?*

PROSPECT: *Well right now, Paul, we don't have a need for any new office furniture.*

SALESPERSON: *How about in the near future?*

PROSPECT: *Ummmm, possibly next spring.*

SALESPERSON: *Who do you usually buy furniture from?*

PROSPECT: *The last time we purchased furniture, it was from Richardson's over on Spring Street.*

SALESPERSON: *How many office staff do you have in your company?*

PROSPECT: *Right now, 45, but that may change after the first of the year.*

SALESPERSON: *Is this your only location?*

PROSPECT: *Yes, but Paul, I don't mean to be rude, but I have a meeting starting in five minutes and I need to cut this short. Why don't you send me your business card and any information you might have on your company . . .*

What buying signals were missed? What was on the salesperson's mind when this call was initiated? Let's look at this call again from a skilled salesperson's perspective.

SALESPERSON: *Stacy, Overbrook is very interested in doing business with your company. Could you tell me how we might make that happen?*

PROSPECT: *Well, right now Paul, we don't have a need for any new office furniture.*

SALESPERSON: *How about in the near future?*

(What does "near future" mean to anyone? Why not, "When do you anticipate that might change?")

PROSPECT: *Ummmm, possibly next spring.*

SALESPERSON: *Who do you usually buy furniture from?*

(Hey, hold on here. What's happening next spring?)

PROSPECT: *The last time we purchased furniture, it was from Richardson's over on Spring Street.*

SALESPERSON: *How many office staff do you have in your company?*

(Slow down. Why did they select Richardson's? What did they buy?)

PROSPECT: *Right now, 45, but that may change after the first of the year.*

SALESPERSON: *Is this your only location?*

(What is bringing about the change after the first of the year? More importantly, will the number of staff be more or less?)

PROSPECT: *Yes, but Paul, I don't mean to be rude but I have a meeting starting in five minutes and I need to cut this short. Why don't you send*

me your business card and any information
you might have on your company . . .

We are much more effective when we have learned to listen first and frame our next question based on what we've just heard. When we listen first, we use good selling skills rather than read from a list of questions.

Most decision makers do not want to talk to salespeople because their questions typically focus on what *they* want to know rather than on what is important or relevant to the prospective customer. We will have much better results when we learn to focus on *their* needs rather than our own. Here is an example of a weak and ineffective telephone prospecting call. See if you can pick up on all the mistakes the salesperson made. Where was he not listening? What buying signals did he miss? When you've made your choices, compare them with our choices that follow.

SALESPERSON: *Jessica, Central Temporary Employment would like to do business with your company. How could we earn the opportunity?*

PROSPECT: *We're currently using another agency for temp services and they do a pretty good job for us.*

SALESPERSON: *Do you have any needs right now?*

PROSPECT: *No. We'll not be needing help until we do our annual fiscal inventory.*

SALESPERSON: *How often do you bring in temporary help?*

PROSPECT: *It varies from month to month, but we depend heavily on temporary help, especially in our busy season.*

SALESPERSON: Does your current agent give you a discount if you want to hire someone for permanent employment?

PROSPECT: Yes, they do, but we're negotiating for a better discount now.

SALESPERSON: Do you only hire temps for the warehouse or do you hire clerical staff too?

PROSPECT: Sometimes. We've had a few occasions where we've needed additional office support. Why don't you just send me your business card and some information about your company . . .

Comparison:

SALESPERSON: Jessica, Central Temporary Employment would like to do business with your company, how could we earn the opportunity?

PROSPECT: We're currently using another agency for temp services and they do a pretty good job for us.

(Only a pretty good job. I would jump on that. How could they do better? I might say, "Jessica, when you say a pretty good job, what would a temp agency need to do for you to say they were doing a great job?")

SALESPERSON: Do you have any needs right now?

PROSPECT: No. We'll not be needing help until we do our annual fiscal inventory.

(Ask when they do their annual fiscal inventory?)

SALESPERSON: How often do you bring in temporary help?

PROSPECT: *It varies from month to month, but we depend heavily on temporary help, especially in our busy season.*

(When are your busiest times?)

SALESPERSON: *Does your current agent give you a discount if you want to hire someone for permanent employment?*

PROSPECT: *Yes, they do, but we're negotiating for a better discount now.*

(Perfect timing. Ask how frequently that happens? What discount are they attempting to get? Let's at least look for some options. Her statement was a "buying signal." This could be our opening.)

SALESPERSON: *Do you only hire temps for the warehouse or do you hire clerical staff too?*

PROSPECT: *Sometimes. We've had a few occasions where we've needed additional office support. Why don't you just send me your business card and some information about your company . . .*

(We could have asked, "What other areas do you find the need for temporary employees?" or, "How do you currently handle any needs you might have for clerical and administrative staff?" The salesperson's question was close-ended.)

This entire conversation could have been much more productive if the salesperson had listened and stayed focused.

There are three primary purposes for fact-finding and qualifying when telephone prospecting:

1. **Determine potential for business.**
2. **Begin building a relationship.**
3. **Develop interest.**

Let's address these one at a time.

1. Determine potential for business.

Every prospect is not a good prospect. Because someone is alive and breathing and willing to meet with you is not a good enough reason to schedule an appointment. How many times have you found yourself sitting across the desk from a prospective customer saying to yourself, "why am I here? This is a waste of my time."

I found myself in that situation alot during my first two years in sales. If anyone was willing to meet with me, I was off and running. I spent time with prospects who could not make the final decision, did not have any money, had no use for the product I sold, or worse, all of the above. I had been trained that nothing was more important than get an appointment, get an appointment, get an appointment.

After a few years, I learned that I had to put a value on my time or I was not going to be successful in sales. To me, successful meant looking at my total earnings at the end of the year with a smile on my face. Most of us would agree the report card of a successful sales professional is their yearly income. Good salespeople use their time wisely. Good salespeople earn above average incomes.

 What are some specific things to watch for when determining potential for business?

 Things you can't control or change.

One example would be the long term relationship that supersedes price, quality, or service. While those types of relationships may be fewer today than in previous years, many still do exist.

Others might include credit risks, unrealistic price expectations, and those who choose to do business locally and won't consider vendors from outside their community.

Whatever the reason, it is up to us to determine if we can justify the time and effort to pursue a lead. In some situations, it may be wiser to move on and look elsewhere. In most situations, we can try again in the future.

2. Begin building a relationship.

In sales, relationships are everything. While socializing with customers and clients can have it benefits, we're not talking about going out with a prospect for a beer and a pizza. We're referring to a professional relationship based on trust and understanding. Not personal friendships, liking each other, having fun, or hanging out together, but relationships based on business respect and communication. What facilitates building those types of relationships? More than anything else we might do, effective fact finding and qualifying.

When I train with sales professionals, I remind them over and over that when you are asking fact finding and qualifying questions in an appropriate and effective manner, you are doing it for them, not you. It's for the prospective client's benefit, not your own.

When prospecting in your particular industry, it's probably not uncommon to regularly hear the same objections, responses, excuses, concerns, and explanations. The prospect, however, does not. Example:

If you sell employee health benefit programs to small businesses, one of your fact-finding and qualifying questions might be: "What is your biggest challenge at this time in providing health benefits to your employees?"

When you ask that question, you will probably hear a variation of the same response 99.9 percent of the time. So why bother to ask the question? Instead of making the assumption and saving time, you ask the question for them, not you. Asking what is important to them is the foundation for building the professional relationship that may lead to a sale. It demonstrates to the prospect that you want to gain an understanding of their needs and concerns.

We know that, as sales professionals, fact finding allows us to determine needs and present the appropriate product or service. In most cases, we can figure that out very quickly. However, when we jump too soon to present a product or service, we may appear as if we only care about making the sale.

We've all heard, "the customer does not care how much you know until they know how much you care."

3. Develop interest.

Not our interest, but their interest. Develop their interest in what we have to say about our product or service.

There is a great sales story that exemplifies "developing interest." I heard it years ago and I've never forgotten it's powerful message.

A young sales professional had a huge sale pending. She was absolutely convinced that she was going to get the contract and earn the biggest commission check her company had ever awarded.

The weekend before the decision was made, she went shopping for a new car. Convinced that within 48 hours she would be driving a new, red sports car, she looked forward to arriving at the office on Monday morning. By late afternoon, the call came from the prospective client. She had not been awarded the contract.

Distraught and feeling low, she walked over to her sales manager and commented, "I guess it's true what they say. You can lead a horse to water but you can't make them drink." The sales manager looked at her and replied, "In sales, it's not your job to make them drink. It's your job to make them thirsty."

If prospecting and developing new business were only about presenting a product, a service or a price, it would be easy. However, it's doing what we need to do to insure the prospective customer wants to do business with us. As our sales manager so aptly stated, "make them thirsty". One of the best ways to insure that happens is through effective fact-finding and qualifying.

Here is an example of how a call might go with a sales professional who has developed effective telephone prospecting skills. Notice how our sales professional uses the techniques we've addressed so far. Look for the salesperson to:

Determine the Decision Maker
Verify the Decision Maker
Ask for the Business
Address the First Point of Resistance (objection)
Begin the Fact-Finding and Qualifying

RECEPTIONIST: *Good morning, Shelby Manufacturing.*

SALESPERSON: *Good morning. This is Don Bates with Marvel Travel Services. I have some information I'd like to forward to the person who would make decisions about corporate travel. Who would that be please?*

RECEPTIONIST: *Probably, Denise Allen.*

SALESPERSON: *And what is Denise's position?*

RECEPTIONIST: *She's Director of Human Resources.*

SALESPERSON: *Would she be available to speak with?*

RECEPTIONIST: *One moment and I'll transfer you to her extension.*

PROSPECT: *Good morning, Denise Allen.*

SALESPERSON: *Good morning Denise. This is Don Bates with Marvel Travel Services. I was told you would be the person who made decisions*

	about corporate travel needs. Have I reached the right person?
PROSPECT:	*Yes.*
SALESPERSON:	*Denise, Marvel would like to work with your company with regard to any travel needs you might have. How could we best earn that opportunity?*
PROSPECT:	*We currently have an agency and they do a good job for us. I see no reason to change.*
SALESPERSON:	*May I ask who you are currently using?*
PROSPECT:	*We use Central Travel Agency and we've been with them for several years.*
SALESPERSON:	*What would have to happen for you to at least consider looking at an alternative agency?*
PROSPECT:	*Probably, most important, is having all arrangements completed correctly and at the best available discount.*
SALESPERSON:	*How do you feel your current agency is doing in those areas now?*
PROSPECT:	*Not bad. There is always room for improvement, but , I'll be honest, I don't think any agency could do any better.*
SALESPERSON:	*Denise, you said there is always room for improvement. Where would you like to see improvements?*

PROSPECT: *I'd like for them to investigate more options. They tend to pick an airline or a hotel chain because it's what the service technician wants and not necessarily where we get the best discount. We try to accommodate our technicians. We know travel can be difficult, but we can't lose money on a project because of travel expenses.*

- How is our sales professional doing?
- Is he listening?
- Are his questions based on what he has heard or is he reading off a list?
- Has he stayed focused?
- How well did he get past the first objection and turn the conversation around?
- Is he beginning to build a relationship and developing interest?
- More importantly, has he learned anything?
- Could you "hear" the sales professional's warm, but assertive manner?

 How will I know when to stop asking questions.

 When you have accomplished one of three objectives.

1. Concluded there is little or no potential for business.
2. The prospect is sending signals indicating "it's time."
3. We've accomplished all we can on this call.

As long as the prospect is responding to your questions, volunteering information, and adding to the conversation, keep going. If you are not sensing they want to terminate the call continue the "appointment." Do what you would be doing if you were sitting across the desk from the prospect instead of talking to them on the telephone. There is no difference.

Remember, the telephone is not a tool to make an appointment, it *is* an appointment.

KEY POINTS FOR CHAPTER FIVE

■ People buy for two primary reasons:
- They trust us.
- They feel we know and understand their needs.

■ Three purposes for fact-finding and qualifying:
- Determine potential for business.
- Begin building a relationship.
- Develop interest.

■ Fact-finding and qualifying questions should be asked in a warm, conversational, and focused manner.

■ Listen. Frame your next question based on what you have just heard.

■ As long as the prospect is responding and contributing to the conversation, keep it going.

Sleep Well When the Hard Winds Blow.

Winnie Ary

The Kiss

6

 When do we get to talk about our company, our product or service?

 Now! It's time for the KISS.

It's now time to ask for the sale or the appointment, whichever is most appropriate in your business. It's now time for the "kiss."

Looking back at where we left off in Chapter Five, let's see how our sales professional might ease into asking for the appointment.

SALESPERSON: *Denise, I would really like to meet with you. If making sure you're company is getting the best available prices is a primary concern, you'll want to see our automated corporate profile program. It shows all travel options that were available at the time of the booking and a copy is included with both your invoice and tickets. I'm confident this is perfect for your needs. What does your schedule look like the first first of next week?*

If we've done everything right to this point, we have a good chance that asking for the appointment will be reasonably well received. If we've stayed focused on the prospect's concerns, needs, and "hot buttons" rather than our own; asked questions in a warm, friendly, and conversational manner; and listened well, we've now earned the right to talk about why our product or service may be the right choice.

We've done the wooing, it's now O.K. to kiss.

Now is the time to utilize all that great product and service expertise we've developed, and because we haven't jumped into those issues too soon, the prospect should be receptive to hearing what we have to say.

The way the sales professional eases into the kiss is another important point. If you recall, our salesperson connected his service to a need he had uncovered during their conversation. He said:

"If making sure you're company is getting the best available price is a primary concern,"

He reinforced he had listened to what was important to the client. Using openings such as:

If that's a concern you might consider our . . .
A benefit in using our company for that service is . . .
Another reason you might consider our . . .
Because your time frames are so tight, the best . . .

I refer to this as "shooting bullets" or giving a specific reason for doing business with us. The alternative is often "shotgunning" or presenting a menu of products or services you offer and hoping something will hit the target.

The prospect needs to see the connection between their need and what we have to offer. This happens only when we have listened well and stayed focused.

Q. Where do we go from here if we were unable to get the appointment or sale?

A. Positioning Ourselves.

During my early years in sales, I had the extreme good fortune to work for an exceptional sales manager. He consistently reinforced his belief that, in sales, positioning was critical. If you are unable to gain an appointment or make the sale on the first attempt, the next best thing is to be well positioned to try again. "Keeping the door open for additional or future attempts is paramount to successful selling" was his battle cry during sales meetings.

Telephone appointments allow for that to happen. You are well positioned when you have developed even a small amount of rapport, and the prospect has gained some understanding of the product or service you represent. If we are not able to achieve all that we hoped for on the first call, we need to work at keeping the door open for subsequent attempts.

There is a thin line that separates persistence from pushy. It's appropriate and often necessary to be persistent, but, never, ever be pushy. When we push too hard on a first telephone prospecting call, we may cause irreparable damage. Pushing too hard or too soon is just not effective in consultative, relationship selling.

Q. What are some ways to insure that you "position" yourself well?

A. Document, document, document.

Today, computerized contact management programs are available by the hundreds. As such, documenting sales calls has become almost hassle free. You can go to any computer store and pick up a contact management program for as little as $39.95 to $299.95.

These software programs will do everything you need and more. What we must capture is the following information:

Who did I talk with?
When did I talk to them?
What did we talk about?
When should I call them again?
Why should I call them again?
What will we talk about when I contact them again?

Think of this as the doctor's appointment book and your medical file being in the same drawer. When the doctor looks at his appointment book and sees that you will be in today for a check-up, he then looks at his notations in your file. In other words, written documentation based on your last visit. With those notes, the doctor is now able to begin a conversation with you starting where he left off the last time you were in his office. That conversation might begin like this:

Melinda, the last time you were in you were having some soreness in your right shoulder. How did that lotion I gave you work?

How does that make Melinda feel? What can this do to build on the relationship, the trust, and the understanding?

Melinda might be saying to herself, I never want to change doctors. I trust mine and he really understands my concerns. That's positioning. Documentation should be used for positioning. It's one of the most important sales tools you have available when telephone prospecting. Document key issues discussed during a telephone appointment and refer back to that information when making subsequent calls. This helps build the kind of relationships that in the past were possible only when meeting face to face.

Our sales professional, Linda Jones, has documented a few telephone prospecting calls to the same potential client. Let's look at how she has used her documentation as a selling tool in each call.

2/13 TT (talked to) Megan Todd, CFO. Lease up Sept. If they move may purchase new telephone equip. w/voice mail. Looking at several properties, all dwntn area. Has 9-year-old Dial-Right w/limited features. 20 stations & maxed out. Wants ability to grow to 40 or more. Fairly receptive to my call, but would not grant an appointment. Sent her info. pkg. Check back 3/2.

On 3/2, this is how Linda began her conversation with Megan?

"Hello Megan, this is Linda Jones with Communications Plus. We spoke a few weeks ago and I wanted to follow-up on the information I sent you. How did the two systems presented in the brochure look to you?"

3/2 TT Megan. Likes the S-22 system, but budget not yet determined. Not sure she can upgrade that much. Still too soon. Wants to wait and see if they will move or stick it out for 2 more yrs. Warming up to me a little. Not real chatty. Still no go on appt. Wants to wait until board meeting April 10 regarding the move. Call back 4/12.

On 4/12 Linda contacts Megan for the third time. Again, following the normal pleasantries, (how are you today, or did you enjoy your weekend, etc.) she uses her documentation as a sales tool to move into a business discussion.

"Megan, I recall you mentioned your board was meeting earlier this week to discuss your upcoming lease expiration? How are things progressing?"

The documentation based on this call is as follows:

4/12 TT Megan. Going to move. Selected Hartman Building dntn. 2 floors. Now has the extra space they need and will look at telephone systems once budget is finalized. Meeting with her Friday, 4/22, to offer suggestions on developing her communications budget. Looks good. Mentioned her vacation. Going to Disney with family in May.

Linda finally got the appointment. Based on Linda's documentation, it does look as if she has done a great job positioning herself. If you remember, she was told no on two occasions when she asked for an appointment, however, she was persistent, not pushy and she used her documentation as a selling tool.

You'll also notice how the prospect appears to begin to build a warmer relationship with Linda by mentioning her family vacation. Let's look at all this one more time.

2/13 TT (talked to) Megan Todd, CFO. Lease up Sept. If they move may purchase new telephone equip. w/voice mail. Looking at several properties, all dwntn area. Has 9-year-old Dial-Right w/limited features. 20 stations & maxed out. Wants ability to grow to 40 or more. Fairly receptive to my call, but would not grant an appointment. Sent her info. pkg. Check back 3/2.

3/2 TT Megan. Likes the S-22 system, but budget not yet determined. Not sure she can upgrade that much. Still too soon. Wants to wait and see if they will move or stick it out for 2 more yrs. Warming up to me a little. Not real chatty. Still no go on appt. Wants to wait until board meeting April 10 regarding the move. Call back 4/12.

4/12 TT Megan. Going to move. Selected Hartman Building dntn. 2 floors. Now has the extra space they need and will look at telephone systems once budget is finalized. Meeting with her Friday, 4/22 , to offer suggestions on developing her communications budget. Looks good. Mentioned vacation. Going to Disney with family in May.

Documentation can be a powerful tool. It's your handshake, your eyes into the prospect's office or workplace. Hypothetically, it places you right there beside the prospect, as if you were having a face to face appointment. It will lead you through the wooing process to the kiss.

CONCLUSION

I'm confident the techniques presented in this book are contrary to what is still being taught by many sales managers today. There are still many companies kicking their sales staff out of the office at 8:30 am in the morning because they believe they should be out on the streets cold calling, door to door. Generally, all that accomplishes is sending them to the nearest coffee shop with all the other salespeople who got kicked out of their offices, or it frustrates them to the degree they give up and move to some other type of employment. As sales professionals, it is so important to recognize the value of building relationships by telephone. It's become almost the preferred way of conducting business, at least in making the initial contact.

Of course we should ask for the appointment, however, asking at the end of the conversation is far less offensive to the prospect than when it's obvious the sole purpose for the telephone call was to get an appointment. Allow time to develop rapport, trust, and understanding. We don't have to kiss on the first date.

Let me leave you with this final thought. There was once a farmer who needed to hire someone to help with the farm chores. During the interviewing process, one young man made such a good impression, the farmer was tempted to offer him the position on the spot. However, the farmer had formed the opinion that most young people were not dependable. When he broached the subject with the young man he was finally persuaded to offer him the position despite a comment he had made which the farmer had not understood. At the risk of appearing naive, the farmer did not ask for an explanation. The young man had said, "I sleep well when the hard winds blow."

A few days after the young man had started working on the farm, and without warning, a terrible blizzard hit the area. The farmer awoke in the middle of the night in a state of panic, confident that his stock and equipment had not been secured to withstand the current weather conditions.

He threw on his clothing and boots and rushed as quickly as he could to the barn only to find that all doors, stalls and shutters had been closed and secured with nails for reinforcement. Extra water, hay, and food had been provided for the livestock, just in case.

The farmer then ran to the equipment shed to check on the tractors, trucks, and tools needed to run the farm and found everything in perfect order. The doors were secured and heavy equipment staked to the pegs in the concrete floor to insure stability. Even the bales of hay had been covered with additional tarps and lines to make sure no damage occurred.

The farmer then walked to the bunk house to check on the young farm hand and found him sound asleep in his bed. Now he knew what the young man meant when he said, "I sleep well when the hard winds blow."

The young man was prepared for his position. His skills were automatic, learned behavior. He did not have to think about what to do when the blizzard was about to hit. He knew what to do. Able to sleep when the winds blew hard, he knew he had done a good job and the results would show.

How well do we sleep when the hard winds blow? Are our prospecting and new business development skills learned behaviors or do we struggle? Mastering the ability to effectively prospect and develop new business will insure for each of us in sales that we will always sleep well when the hard winds blow.

GOOD LUCK AND GOOD SELLING.

Tips to Aid in Developing Your Telephone Prospecting Skills

1. Practice in private.

Initially, most of us are not comfortable making telephone prospecting calls if others are listening. Find a private office or area where you can make calls and practice your skills until you are comfortable with what you are doing and saying.

2. Tape your calls.

Telephone recording devices are available at places like Radio Shack or Hello Direct Catalogs. (Taping a two-way conversation is generally not illegal if you are one of the two people on the call and no one else is going to hear the tape.) Tape record some of your prospecting calls.

After taping, listen to and critique your calls.

Did I make sure I was addressing the appropriate decision maker?
Did I speak in an assertive but warm and friendly manner?
Was I focused and asking questions in a conversational manner?
Did I leave the door open for subsequent calls?
Where do I need to focus for improvement?

Tape recording your calls is the single most effective way to improve your telephone prospecting skills. If you are sensitive to taping both ends of the conversation, record only your side. That is what is most important anyway.

3. Set goals.

Pick specific skills we've addressed in the book and set a date to have them be "learned behaviors." Work to improve your skills to the degree that you no longer need to think about what you are going to say. When that happens, you have mastered the skills.